HEATHROW

JONATHAN FALCONER

LONDON

IAN ALLAN LTD

First published 1990

ISBN 0 7110 1939 8

Published by Ian Allan Ltd, Shepperton, Surrey; and printed by Ian Allan Printing Ltd at their works at Coombelands in Runnymede, England

Previous page:
Tails of an airport: Heathrow's Terminal 2 apron.
BAA/Arthur Kemsley

Right:
Heathrow is home to British Airways, the UK's principal national carrier. Boeing 747-236B G-BDXA is one of over 20 Series 200s operated by the airline on long-haul routes.
BAA/Arthur Kemsley

Introduction

Since the Lockerbie tragedy when, on 21 December 1988, Pan Am Flight 103 was blown apart by a terrorist bomb over Scotland, airport security in the Western world has been tightened considerably.

One of the side effects of this new security has been severely to curtail photography on and around airport property. Long gone are the accommodating days of the 1950s when one could stroll on to the apron at Heathrow and snap Stratocruisers and Connies as they were being turned around. Sadly, the many opportunities for legitimate photography which existed up until a few years ago have, like the Stratocruisers and Connies, vanished along with many of the values of a bygone age.

The aim of this book has been to give a general photographic impression of the many aircraft types using Heathrow Airport — both 'then' and 'now'. We are fortunate that, through the lenses of the likes of Gerald Robinson, Anthony Wirkus and Peter Cooper, there is a strong photographic record of Heathrow in colour since the sixties. It is unlikely, however, that this breadth of photographic coverage will be possible to record the Heathrow of the nineties.

Due to limited availability of suitable colour material and limited access to the airside at Heathrow, it has been impossible to record every type of aircraft using the airport. But what has been achieved in the limited scope of 64 pages is, I believe, an impression of Heathrow — the world's premier international airport.

Acknowledgements

I should like to thank the following people and organisations for the assistance they gave during the writing of this book: Peter Norton, British Airways Engineering; John Silver, British Airways Public Relations; Capt Geoffrey Shaw, Beecham International Aviation Ltd; Field Aviation (Heathrow) Ltd; David Towler, British Airways AERAD; Carol Saunders and Amanda Poole, Heathrow Airport Ltd, Public Relations Department; Terry Quantrill, Public Relations Officer, National Air Traffic Services, Heathrow; Peter Kennedy, CAA Public Relations; Alan J. Wright for his help in checking the manuscript.

The following people have also helped immeasurably through providing many of the photographs reproduced on the pages that follow: Arthur Kemsley of BAA; Robbie Shaw; Gerald Robinson; Bill Blanchard; Allan Burney; Anthony Wirkus and Colin Addison.

Jonathan Falconer
Shepperton
October 1989

Front cover:
An atmosphere of tasteful opulence pervades the British Airways Speedwing Lounge at Terminal 4 where passengers for Concorde and First Class intercontinental subsonic flights can relax before boarding. Passengers can watch through the panoramic blind-draped windows as Concorde is readied for departure. *Jonathan Falconer*

Back cover:
Crabbing slightly in the fresh southwesterly wind, Swissair A310-221 HB-IPE passes over the ILS localiser at the head of Runway 27R . . . seconds from touchdown with an afternoon flight from Geneva. *Allan Burney*

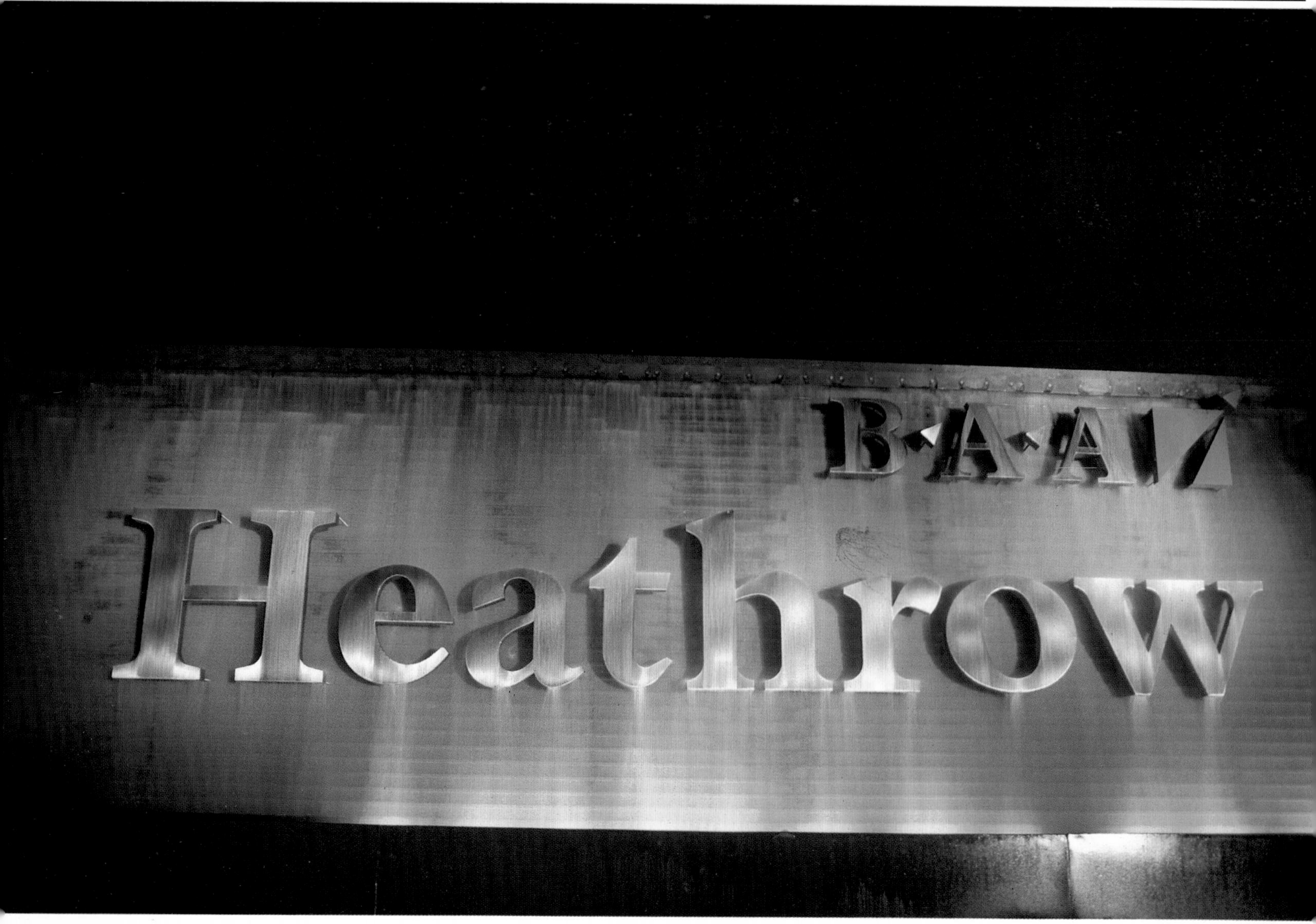
BAA
Heathrow

Heathrow Airport

Love them or loathe them, airports are very much an integral and accepted part of 20th century lifestyle, and there can be few people today who have not set foot inside an airport terminal or flown in an aeroplane at some point in their lives.

People moving is big business. In the year 1988-89 alone, over 68 million terminal passengers (that is, passengers joining or leaving an aircraft) passed through Britain's seven BAA-owned airports, and more than half this number used Heathrow — the world's premier international airport and the largest of London's four airports. But people moving is not the only source of revenue for airports and airlines: in the same period Heathrow handled 656,107 tonnes of air freight in both passenger and all-cargo aircraft.

Heathrow and its environs are no strangers to travellers. Centuries before the advent of the aeroplane, the Bath Road — which today forms the northern boundary of the airport — was a major coaching route between London and the West Country resort city of Bath. Hounslow Heath, much of which now lies beneath the airport and its surrounding suburban sprawl, had to be crossed by stage coaches on their way west, but it was a lonely and dangerous place. The important coaching centre of Hounslow marked the end of the first stage out of the Capital, and the opportunity for a change of horses before the dash across the Heath towards the comparative safety of Colnbrook and Slough. In rainy weather mud often lay up to two feet deep on the Heath which also offered plenty of ideal cover for highwaymen who made a fat living from holding up passing coaches. As late as 1800, some 13 gibbets stood along the road from Hounslow to Heston, a distance of two miles, as a sobering deterrent to would-be robbers.

The aviation history of the area now known as Heathrow Airport actually began in 1929 when the Fairey Aviation Co Ltd purchased a 150-acre area of land near Harmondsworth, just to the northeast of Stanwell in Middlesex. A private aerodrome — known variously as Harmondsworth, or the Great West Aerodrome, and later as Heathrow — was laid out and used as Fairey's flight testing centre. It remained in use until requisitioned by the Air Ministry in 1944 when the site was found suitable for the construction of a bomber airfield using the triangular runway system then favoured. Fairey's was offered alternative accommodation and moved to Heston which had been specially developed. However, peace broke out before the airfield at Heathrow could be put to military use and so it was decided to re-plan it for civil operations.

A committee of experts was convened to decide on the development and their decisions resulted in the runway pattern known as the 'Star of David' which enabled aircraft to take off and land in any possible wind direction. By the end of 1945 the first runway and some rather rudimentary buildings had been completed and on 1 January 1946 the site was officially handed over by the Air Ministry to the civil authorities. The first commercial aircraft to use the new London (Heathrow) Airport was Avro Lancastrian G-AGWG *Star Light* of British South American Airways on 1 December. On New Year's Day 1946 she embarked on a route-proving flight to Buenos Aires piloted by Donald Bennett, wartime commander of the RAF's legendary Pathfinder Force. By March BSAA was flying two services a week to South America, the single journey taking some 24hr.

Two months later on 28 May, BOAC's first regular service out of Heathrow was flown by a Lancastrian to Karachi. From this point — but later from Singapore — Qantas crews took over to complete the 'Kangaroo' route to Sydney. The basic passenger fare for this trip was £220 single. Today it costs £680.

By 1947, all three runways in the first triangle of the Star of David had been completed and work progressed on the second triangle phase. By 1950 the runway layout was almost complete but work on Runway 3 had been halted in order to facilitate the construction work underway in the Central Area. A plan for a permanent terminal complex was drawn up and in 1950 Heathrow Airport as we know it today began to take shape. Armies of construction workers then moved into the centre of the airport and work began on a new control tower, two short-haul passenger buildings — one for continental traffic known as No 1 Building EUROPA, and one for domestic traffic known as No 2 Building BRITANNIC; both buildings now form Terminal 2. A red brick and glass building to house the airport's administrative functions (Queen's Building) was also constructed.

Far left:
Welcome to Heathrow!
Jonathan Falconer

Far right:
The graceful lines of intercontinental Lockheed Constellations were a familiar sight at Heathrow during the 1940s, 1950s and 1960s, but by the time this photograph was taken on 19 April 1969, echoes of the 'Connie' and its Wright Turbo Compound radials had begun to fade, drowned by the advent of the jet age.

Pictured here in the markings of French cargo airline Catair, Super Constellation L-1049G F-BHMI was originally one of 14 L-1049Gs operated by Air France. *Gerald Robinson*

On 31 October 1954 Northolt Airport, the RAF airfield four miles north of Heathrow, was closed to scheduled civil airline operators having been on loan to the Ministry of Civil Aviation from the Air Ministry since 1 February 1946. It had previously handled the regular DC-3 operated services of BOAC's European Division (which became BEA on 1 August) to Paris, Brussels, Amsterdam, Helsinki, Madrid and Stockholm, and also those of several foreign operators. These services and BEA's maintenance operation were transferred to Heathrow, more than doubling the airport's passenger and aircraft movements.

The inauguration of the first three permanent buildings in the Central Area on 16 December 1955 signalled the end of the first phase of permanent building. In this the era of Constellations and Stratocruisers, it soon became apparent with the steady increase in passengers that the existing facilities could soon become inadequate: in the year up to 28 December 1956 Heathrow handled three million passengers whilst by comparison Northolt had handled almost five million in the period 1946-54.

The Millbourn Report published on 1 August 1957 proposed a new layout for the Central Area with three main recommendations: the construction of a second short-haul terminal (Terminal 1), a new long-haul terminal (Terminal 3), and a cargo building to be constructed parallel to the No 1 Runway (now 09L/27R). However, with the rapid growth in the air freight business this last proposal was abandoned and the cargo terminal was eventually built on the south side of the airport, opening in December 1968.

The second short-haul terminal was opened on 6 November 1968 as Terminal 1, whilst the long-haul terminal (known as the No 3 Building OCEANIC, and now Terminal 3) was completed and in operation by 1961 for long distance intercontinental flights. By this stage all of Heathrow's passenger terminals were equipped with pier and air-jetty systems for passenger boarding.

Throughout the 1960s and 1970s, the number of passengers using the airport continued to grow, rising to 26,572,631 by 1978-79. It became increasingly apparent that Heathrow would be required to handle more of the new generation of wide-bodied aircraft like the Boeing 747, McDonnell Douglas DC-10 and Lockheed TriStar. To cater for this trend the existing Terminal 3 building was converted to be used solely for departures, and a new arrivals building was opened in 1970. In the late 1980s, wide-bodied aircraft represented 25% of Heathrow's air traffic movements, but carried nearly 50% of its passengers. The year 1981 saw the opening of Eurolounge, basically a large gateroom connecting Terminals 1 and 2, and used primarily as a waiting area for up to 700 passengers on the high density European routes. In August 1983 Terminal 1's international pier was reopened to passengers after an £11 million redevelopment. Since then many improvements have been made to all three terminals in response to passenger traffic demands. April 1986 saw the opening of the new £200 million Terminal 4, designed for a mix of short and long-haul traffic and the capacity to handle eight million passengers a year at a rate of 4,000 per hour.

During the same period efforts were made to improve the airport's links with the Capital. The opening of a spur from the M4 motorway to Heathrow's Central Area in March 1965 considerably reduced road journey time from Central London. In 1971 work started on a 3½-mile double-track extension to London Underground's Piccadilly Line from its terminus at Hounslow West to the Central Area in December 1977, linked to each of the three Central Area terminals by moving walkways. Within a week of opening, up to 24,000 passengers a day were being carried by Underground to and from the heart of the airport with a journey time of 47min from the West End.

As an interim measure pending completion of the M25 London Orbital motorway linking Heathrow and Gatwick, an inter-airport helicopter service was inaugurated by HRH The Prince of Wales on 9 June 1978. Known as the Gatwick-Heathrow Airlink, the service utilised a 28-passenger Sikorsky S-61N helicopter operated by BCal in association with British Airports Authority and British Airways Helicopters, making 10 round trips each day for domestic passengers and travellers connecting between European flights. The service was timed to coincide with the morning and afternoon peak periods at both airports.

However, the attraction of the helicopter as a convenient means of transferring passengers to and from Heathrow had been explored during 1955. An experimental and short-lived service was operated by BEA using seven-seat Sikorsky S-55 helicopters linking Heathrow with the South Bank Air Station near Waterloo BR station.

The opening of the M25 section between Reigate and Wisley in October 1985 was followed by the introduction of the nonstop 'Speedlink' coach service linking Heathrow and Gatwick; consequently, Airlink helicopter flights ceased on 6 February 1986.

Heathrow in the 1990s

Heathrow today is one of seven British airports owned by BAA PLC (formerly the British Airports Authority) and is operated by Heathrow Airport Ltd (HAL) which is responsible for the provision,

maintenance and development of passenger terminals, buildings, roads and car parks; and the provision of airfield resources for aircraft operations. In a round-the-clock operation, 365 days a year, some 66 airlines link the airport with 213 destinations in 84 countries served by direct flights, and there are also several dedicated cargo airlines.

The winning combination of more experience in handling international passengers, a high frequency of flights to a multitude of destinations, zoned passport control to ease passenger flows, easy terminal transfers and convenient links to Central London and major UK cities and towns by Underground and express coach services respectively, make Heathrow the world's premier international airport.

It now handles some 38 million passengers a year in over 330,000 aircraft movements using four passenger terminals — three in the Central Area and the fourth with separate road and Underground connections. The Heathrow World Cargo Centre in the southeast corner of the airport is instrumental in the handling of much of the annual 656,000 tonnes of cargo and 67,000 tonnes of mail that currently pass through the airport (1988-89 figures).

To facilitate this massive throughput in people and cargo, the airport uses three runways: 09L/27R (12,800ft×150ft), 09R/27L (12,000ft×150ft) which run parallel to each other are classed as the main runways. Runway 05/23 (7,734ft×150ft) is aligned diagonally along a NE/SW axis and is only used when there is a strong wind blowing from the southwest, or when the crosswind component on the main runways exceeds 20kt. To minimise the discomfort caused by aircraft noise to people living close to the airport, the two main runways for taking off and landing during westerly operations are alternated each day. At exactly 3pm the landing and take-off pattern is switched around so that no single area beneath the flight path suffers for the whole day.

For passenger boarding and freight loading the airport offers a total of 162 aircraft parking stands: 112 in the Central Area with 62 of these capable of taking wide-bodied aircraft; 23 at Terminal 4 with 21 large enough to accommodate wide-bodied aircraft; and 25 at the World Cargo Centre where 16 are able to take wide-bodied aircraft. The allocation of all 162 parking stands to the right aircraft at the correct terminal at the right time is a complicated operation, especially if one considers that up to 80 aircraft take off or land each hour during peak periods. In fact, during the busiest day in 1988 (16 September) some 1,121 aircraft movements were recorded.

To keep all of these aircraft on the move the fuelling operation at Heathrow is a highly complex affair. From 361,660sq ft of storage tanks at Perry Oaks at the airport's western end, a network of underground pipelines carrying JET-A1 aviation fuel is connected to hydrants at parking stands where dispenser vehicles form the final link in the fuelling chain to the aircrafts' fuel tanks. To give some idea of the vast quantities of fuel dealt with in fuelling operations, the total quantity of aviation fuel supplied to aircraft at Heathrow in 1986 was some 650 million gallons.

Terminal 1

In 1988 Terminal 1 handled more than 13.5 million passengers and is the busiest of the four passenger terminals at Heathrow. It can also boast the highest proportion of regular travellers, particularly on domestic services where some passengers fly several times a week. Arrivals are on the ground floor, departures on the upper level.

Twelve airlines currently use Terminal 1, operating a mixture of short, medium and long-haul routes: Aer Lingus (B737, BAC One-Eleven), Air UK (BAe 146, Shorts 360), British Airways (UK Shuttle and Europe, not Paris and Amsterdam; B737, 757, 767, L1011, BAC One-Eleven, A320), British Midland Airways (DC-9, BAe ATP, Shorts 360, B737), Brymon Airways (DHC Dash-7), Cyprus Airways (A310, B707), Dan-Air (B737, BAC One-Eleven), El Al (B747, 757, 767), Icelandair (B727, DC-8), Manx Airlines (BAe 146, ATP, Shorts 360), Sabena Belgian Airlines (B737, FH-227, Fellowship), and South African Airways (B747).

Terminal 2

The airport's oldest passenger terminal building, today Terminal 2 houses 22 airlines operating short and medium-haul services to over 80 direct destinations in Europe and is used by approximately eight million passengers a year. Check-in is on the ground floor immediately on entering the building, whilst on the first floor are the passenger arrival and departure points. Terminal 2 is linked to Terminal 1 by a walkway for transfers to domestic flights. Airlines currently using Terminal 2 include: Aeroflot (Tu-154, Il62/86), Air Algerie (B727/737), Air France (A300/310, B727/737, ATR42, Fellowship, SF340), Alitalia (DC-9, MD-80, A300), Austrian Airlines (MD-80), Balkan Bulgarian Airlines (Tu-154), CSA Czechoslovak Airlines (Il-62, Tu-154), Finnair (DC-9, MD-80), Iberia (DC-9, B727, A300, DC-10), JAT Yugoslav Airlines (DC-9, B727/737), LOT Polish Airlines (Tu-134/154, Il-62), Lufthansa (A310, B727/737), Luxair

(Friendship, Fokker 50, B737) Malev Hungarian Airlines (Tu-134/154), Olympic Airways (A310, B727), Royal Air Maroc (B727/737/757), SAS (DC-9, MD-80), Swissair (MD-80, A310, Fokker 100), TAP Air Portugal (B727/737, L1011), Tarom Romanian (BAC One-Eleven, Tu-154), Tunis Air (B727), and THY Turkish Airlines (A310, B727).

Terminal 3

Terminal 3's £110 million phased reconstruction programme begun in 1986 was completed in May 1990. Its purpose was to create larger passenger handling areas, particularly check-ins (134 new check-in desks in Departures equipped with the latest automated baggage sorting facilities); to rationalise passenger flow routes; to expand commercial facilities and to generally modernise the terminal. The terminal now will be able to handle approximately 3,000 departing passengers and 3,200 arriving passengers per hour.

Terminal 3 handles long-haul intercontinental flights with the exception of British Airways which is now in Terminal 4.

Thirty airlines use the terminal today: Air Canada (B747/767, L1011), Air India (B747), Air Mauritius (B747/767), Alia Royal Jordanian Airlines (A310, L1011), Bangladesh Biman (DC-10), BWIA International (L1011), Egyptair (A300), Ethiopian Airlines (B767), Ghana Airways (DC-10), Gulf Air (B767, L1011), Iran Air (B747SP), Iraqi Airways (B727, 747), Japan Airlines (B747), Kenya Airways (A310), Kuwait Airways (B747), Malaysian Airline System (B747, DC-10), Middle East Airlines (B707), Nigeria Airways (A310, B747, DC-10), Pakistan International Airlines (B747), Pan American World Airways (B727/747, A310), Qantas (B747), Saudia-Saudi Arabian Airlines (B747), Singapore Airlines (B747), Sudan Airways (A310), Syrian Arab Airlines (B747), Thai International (B747), Trans World Airlines (B747/767, L1011), VARIG Brazilian Airlines (B747, DC-10), VIASA Venezuelan Airlines (DC-10), and Zambia Airways (DC-10).

Terminal 4

Opened to traffic on 12 April 1986, some 7.5 million passengers used the terminal in the 12 months to March 1989. With the opening of Terminal 4, British Airways moved its long-haul operation — including Concorde flights — from Terminal 3, and its Paris and Amsterdam traffic from Terminal 1. At the same time it was joined at Terminal 4 by KLM Royal Dutch Airlines, NLM CityHopper (a subsidiary of KLM), and Air Malta from Terminal 2.

Built on a 173-acre site in the southeast corner of the airport, away from the Central Area, Terminal 4 is recognised as a world leader in airport terminal design and offers 72 check-in desks and 17 aircraft gates. Departures are on the first floor and arrivals on the ground floor — passenger segregation being one of the major keys to the terminal's success. A 3½-mile extension to the Piccadilly Line from Hatton Cross links Terminal 4 to Heathrow Central with a single-track loop.

Heathrow World Cargo Centre

As well as being the UK's largest passenger airport, Heathrow is also the country's premier air cargo handling facility. The 576,309 tonnes of cargo that passed through the airport in 1987 represented 13.7% of visual trade through all British ports, and 72.8% through all UK airports.

Situated in the southwest corner of the airport and covering an area of 160 acres, Heathrow World Cargo Centre is linked directly to the Central Area passenger terminals by a road tunnel under Runway 09R/27L, and with a spur to Terminal 4. Significant use is made of the tunnel as over 80% of Heathrow's air cargo is moved in the holds of scheduled passenger aircraft.

Of the 23 aircraft stands at the Cargo Centre, eight can handle Boeing 747s, with 11 large and four smaller stands. All-cargo operators with regular schedules are Federal Express which took over Flying Tiger Line's aircraft and operations in August 1989 (Boeing 747-200F, DC-10-10, DC-10-30), and Tunis Air (Boeing 707-320F). Some 20 scheduled cargo carriers and up to 40 non-scheduled operators also use the Cargo Centre.

The Cargo Centre has some 337,260sq ft of bonded transit shed space, built and owned mainly by 16 airlines on land leased from Heathrow Airport Ltd.

General Aviation

Situated on the airport's southside, adjacent to Terminal 4, the General Aviation centre provides facilities for private non-scheduled aircraft. Owing to London's pre-eminence as a centre of finance and commerce, a great number of foreign executive, government and VIP aircraft use Heathrow, coming mainly from Europe, North America and the Middle East. During 1988-89, some 18,100 general aviation flights used the airport.

After arrival at Heathrow, executive jets and turboprops from outside the UK are allocated a Central Area stand for the purposes of customs clearance and other formalities before being towed to their designated parking areas.

There are two main aircraft handling agents for general aviation at Heathrow, and these are British Airways Executive Services, and Field Aircraft Services Ltd. Aircraft making use of the former are

usually to be found parked at British Airways' maintenance base at Hatton Cross; while those which make use of the latter can be seen on the southside of the airport. Government and VIP aircraft are usually parked beside the VIP lounge which is adjacent to the Cargo Centre. Heathrow also has helicopter landing facilities which are situated on the airport's southside.

British Airways

With one of the most comprehensive route networks of any airline, British Airways uses Heathrow Airport as its home base. As the primary national flag carrier, the airline's principal business is the operation of international, domestic scheduled and charter flights for the carriage of passengers, cargo and mail. In addition to the airline's comprehensive administration and training facilities, the airport also plays host to British Airway's Cargo Business Centre at the southside and a 220-acre engineering base at Hatton Cross where some 25 aircraft per day on average pass through the hangars. In addition to engineering support for the airline's fleet of over 200 aircraft, British Airways also undertakes contract servicing of aircraft for the Ministry of Defence and other airlines such as South African Airways and Virgin Atlantic.

Air Traffic Control

Operated by the Civil Aviation Authority (CAA), Heathrow's Air Traffic Control Tower in the Central Area overlooks the airport's terminals and runways. From the tower's 120ft vantage point, air traffic controllers supervise approximately 500 incoming aircraft per day with a similar number requiring take-off clearance. During 1989 the existing Approach and Visual Control Rooms were completely refurbished in a £7 million re-equipment programme. Approach Control was relocated on the ground floor as a result of the refurbishment; it had been previously situated on the floor beneath the Visual Control Room. The latest radar processing and display system has been installed whilst upstairs in the VCR new purpose-built consoles and the latest information displays have been fitted. These will provide controllers with the airport information necessary to sequence and control arriving and departing aircraft. A new Plessey Watchman approach control radar has also been installed together with a new ground movement radar supplied by Thomson CSF. With the forecast of a steady increase in aircraft movements in coming years, these new facilities and equipment will assist air traffic controllers to handle safely and efficiently the growth in air traffic.

Future Developments

The face of Heathrow has changed almost beyond recognition in the 40-odd years since it began operations after World War 2. And it is likely to change even further in the coming years if it is to maintain its position as the world's premier international airport.

With an ever-growing number of passengers and aircraft using the London airports, existing terminal facilities will eventually prove inadequate. Still more terminal capacity is likely to be required by the late 1990s in order to cope with the increased traffic. The Perry Oaks site at the western end of Heathrow has been tipped as a likely site for a fifth terminal, although there are no firm plans at the time of writing.

British Midland, the second largest UK scheduled airline, has plans to develop a new hangar and maintenance area on a five-acre site at the airport, capable of accommodating the largest aircraft in commercial service including the Boeing 747-400. Due to be commissioned in 1991, the maintenance hangar will have an area of 63,000sq ft and will give British Midland the facilities it needs to expand its operations into the long-haul market, and to compete with British Airways in its contract engineering and maintenance operation.

In July 1988 the Dept of Transport accepted a joint BAA/British Rail scheme for a high speed, nonstop rail service linking Heathrow with Paddington station in west London. The result of the Heathrow Surface Access Study of 1987, it is anticipated that the link can be brought into service in 1993. BAA's plans include constructing an electrified branch line from Stocley to Heathrow, a tunnel under the airport, two stations in the Central Area and one at Terminal 4, and the provision of rolling stock.

A $45 million improvement scheme for Terminal 1 began in the spring of 1990, including a new lounge for passengers on Republic of Ireland and Channel Island flights, new facilities for passengers to Belfast and improvements in facilities for those on domestic flights. The number of pier-served aircraft gates for domestic flights will be increased from nine to 18.

Far left:
Of note as being the first Russian jet airliner — and only the second jet airliner type to enter regular airline service — the Tupolev Tu-104 first entered service with Aeroflot on 15 September 1956. Tu-104B CCCP42403 is pictured on finals at Heathrow on 11 May 1973.
Gerald Robinson

This page:

Then and now: the Rolls-Royce Spey-powered Hawker Siddeley Trident was one of the noisier and more common short/medium-haul jet transport types to frequent Heathrow from the early 1960s, although not endearing itself to those unfortunate enough to live under its flightpath.

Northeast Airlines' Trident 1E G-AVYC (inset), pictured here on 7 May 1972, was one of several operated by this wholly-owned subsidiary of BEA on UK domestic services to Newcastle and Leeds/Bradford (amongst others) from Heathrow. Northeast became a subsidiary of British Airways in July 1973, although the aircraft continued to carry Northeast titles until March 1976. The Trident as a type soldiered on for another 13 years, finally retiring from BA's service in 1985.

However, 'Yankee-Charlie' (main picture) seen here in May 1981, did not live to see out the end of the Trident age, but suffered the indignity of being broken up in BA's back yard. *Gerald Robinson/Peter J. Cooper*

The Vickers Viscount made history in being the first ever turbine-powered airliner to carry fare-paying passengers and eventually became one of the best-selling British commercial transport aircraft. During 1967 British Midland introduced the Viscount on domestic services from Heathrow and its home base of East Midlands Airport, represented here by 'stretched' V836 Viscount G-BFZL (now owned by British Air Ferries at Southend). In the background can be seen an unidentified Series 800 Viscount belonging to British Airways. *Anthony Wirkus*

This page:

Push-back: Sudan Airways' slender Comet 4C ST-AAX begins the first leg of its ground manoeuvring at Heathrow before taking the air en route to Khartoum, on 5 August 1972. With the introduction of the Comet 4C in 1963, Sudan Airways was able to expand its route network and frequency of flights on international services. *Gerald Robinson*

Right:

Boeing's 707 was the first commercial jet airliner built by the USA; its 707-320 Combi version could carry a mixed payload of passengers and cargo. Two frequent users of Heathrow's Terminal 3 during the 1970s were Kuwait Airways' Boeing 707-369C 9K-ACM, and British Airways' 707-379C G-AWHU (built originally for US carrier Saturn as N762U, but delivered instead to BOAC on 27 June 1968), pictured here on a wet November day in 1977. *Anthony Wirkus*

Far left:
Heathrow by night, viewed from the northern perimeter.
Jonathan Falconer

Left:
In recent years the string of hotels that have sprung up along the northern perimeter of the airport have become familiar landmarks, as well as relieving Heathrow passengers of over £80 million a year. Here the 569-bedroom Post House Hotel acts as a backdrop for Alitalia'a DC-9-82 I-DAWD. *Allan Burney*

Above:

All roads lead to Heathrow — or so it would seem. The airport has over 40 miles of roads and covers some 2,958 acres, while the perimeter road itself is 9½ miles long. *Jonathan Falconer*

Right:

A free bus service connects all four terminals while some 60 long and short distance scheduled bus and coach services link Heathrow with destinations nationwide. *Jonathan Falconer*

Far right:

Twenty-two foreign airlines currently operate from Terminal 2. It is from the public viewing area on top of the Queen's Building that visitors to the airport can observe arrivals and departures from Piers 1 and 2, although for photographers this is a far from ideal viewpoint due to its situation in relation to the movement of the sun.

Four flights a week to Faro in Portugal are flown by TAP using Boeing 727-200s. *Jonathan Falconer*

Right:
Feverish activity surrounds the arrival of Air France's A300-B2 F-GBEC at Terminal 2 on 14 February 1990. *Jonathan Falconer*

Far right:
Late afternoon sunshine slants across the airport's eastern inner ring road in the Central Area. To the left is Terminal 2, the airport's oldest passenger terminal. Since its opening in 1955 the building has been continually updated to keep abreast of burgeoning demand and now offers many improvements to streamline passenger flows. On the taxi rank outside the terminal building can be seen a few of the 3,000 taxis that pass through Heathrow's taxi feeder park each day. To the right can be seen the base of the Control Tower building and in the far background Terminal 3's Pier 6 and the entrance to the cargo tunnel. *Jonathan Falconer*

Far left:

From Heathrow with love: having obtained clearance for pushback and startup from Heathrow Ground, Lufthansa Boeing 737-230 D-ABHM is pushed back from its parking stand at Terminal 2 on St Valentine's Day 1990, with a flight to Bremen.
Jonathan Falconer

Left:

From its unique vantage point in the Central Area of the airport, controllers in Heathrow tower's Visual Control Room (VCR) enjoy an unspoilt 360° panoramic view of the whole airport. On the raised structure to the right of the VCR is the Aerodrome Surface Movement Indicator radar scanner.
Jonathan Falconer

Far left:
On completion of pushback the Ground Engineer calls the Pilot, using his ground headset connected to the aircraft by a wanderlead, to apply the aircraft's parking brake before the towbar is disconnected. Boeing 737-330 D-ABXF sports Lufthansa's new livery adopted in 1989. *Jonathan Falconer*

Left:
Visual Control: in the glazed VCR on top of the 120ft high Control Tower can be found the Ground Movement Planner (GMP), Ground Movement Controller (GMC), Air Arrivals Controller (AAC), and Air Departures Controller (ADC), aided by a number of Control Assistants.

The time is 11.45am on Monday 4 September 1989: Controllers of 'D' Watch man the VCR. Runways in operation this morning are 27L for arrivals and 27R for departures. Visibility is good today: from this lofty vantage point not only does one have a panoramic view of the airport, but one can also see Windsor Castle to the west, the Telecom Tower to the northeast, and the Crystal Palace transmitter mast to the east. In the foreground sits the assistant to the GMC and GMP, whilst in the background and to the right can be seen the AAC and ADC. *Jonathan Falconer*

Right:

Pilot's eye view of Heathrow: in the foreground can be seen the Southern Perimeter Road and Terminal 4; Runway 09R/27L bisected by Runway 05/23; the Central Area Terminals 1, 2 and 3; and Runway 09L/27R. *Arthur Kemsley/BAA*

Far right:

Boeing 757s accounted for approximately 14½% of air traffic movements at Heathrow during 1988-89, second only in popularity to its twin-jet sister, the 737. Flagship of British Airways' European fleet, the 757 entered service with the airline in February 1983 and is scheduled to fly domestic Super Shuttle services, and to over 20 destinations in Europe, Scandinavia and North Africa. G-BKRM was leased from Air Europe during 1988 to augment BA's fleet. *Peter J. Cooper*

Right:

Approach Control: arriving flights are generally directed by the London Air Traffic Control Centre (LATCC) at West Drayton to route via one of the four holding points as part of the Standard Arrival Route (STAR). These are at Lambourne (northeast), Bovingdon (north), Ockham (south) and at Biggin (southeast). As the flight approaches one of the holding points, LATCC instructs the pilot to contact Heathrow Approach where controllers direct aircraft from the northern and southern holding points so that they are formed into flows of traffic approaching the landing runway. Traffic is then merged into one stream of regularly spaced flights in line with the landing runway where they are fully established on to the Instrument Landing System (ILS) prior to touchdown.

In the soft semi-darkness of the new Approach Control Room on the groundfloor of the Control Tower building, controllers of 'D' Watch use radar to guide aircraft for their final approach. The Approach Control function is due to be transferred to LATCC in 1991, although the Heathrow facility will remain as a back-up.

Jonathan Falconer

Left:

**A Tale of Several Cities: framed
by the tailplane of Air France
Airbus A300B4 F-BVGR,
Norwegian SAS DC-9-41 LN-RLD
is typical of the many
Scandinavian DC-9 twinjets that
are frequent visitors to
Terminal 2. The Air France
Airbus is also typical of the
many overseas types which
operate frequent daily services
from the airport to the key cities
of Europe. Some 30 flights a day
are scheduled to Paris alone,
many of which are flown by the
Airbus family of wide-bodies.**
BAA/Arthur Kemsley

Far left and left:
Crabbing slightly in the fresh southwesterly wind, Swissair A310-221 HB-IPE passes over the ILS localiser at the head of Runway 27R . . . seconds from touchdown with an afternoon flight from Geneva. *Allan Burney*

Right:

Finland's national carrier Finnair is the world's fifth oldest airline: it operates an extensive network of international scheduled services from Helsinki including a thrice-daily (1989) service to Heathrow using MD-80 and DC-9 equipment. Finnair's pristine MD-82 OH-LMO is pictured from the 'business' end at Terminal 2 on 12 April 1989. *Jonathan Falconer*

Centre right:

Pictured at British Airways' Engineering base on 11 January 1989, Airbus A310-300 V8-HM1 is finished in the markings of Royal Brunei Airlines and acts as a VIP transport for the Sultan and his ministers.
Jonathan Falconer

Far right:

The light of a setting winter sun gilds the tailplane of TWA's Boeing 747-284B N305TW as it manoeuvres into position on holding point 112 at the head of Runway 09L to await take-off clearance. In the background, Swissair's Airbus A310-221 HB-IPA prepares to line up as soon as N305TW has headed down the runway.

 Wide-bodied aircraft like the Airbus carry approximately 50% of Heathrow's passenger throughput annually.
Jonathan Falconer

Gulf Air's network of scheduled passenger and cargo services reach across the miles to link the Gulf State of Bahrain with Heathrow. Formed in March 1950, Gulf Air's shares are held by the governments of the Gulf States of Bahrain, Oman, Qatar and the United Arab Emirates.

On finals to Runway 27R and only seconds from touchdown, the elegant shape of L-1011-385 TriStar 200 N92TB typifies the fleet of nine operated by the airline into Terminal 3.
Bill Blanchard

Left:
A twice-weekly direct service to the Ghanaian capital Accra is flown by Ghana Airways' sole DC-10-30, 9G-ANA, pictured here at the head of Runway 09R and about to begin her take-off run. *Allan Burney*

Above and right:
Where Orient meets Occident: the new fleet liveries adopted by Japan Air Lines and Lufthansa during 1989-90 display a striking similarity. Both Lufthansa's A310-203 D-AICD and JAL's Boeing 747-146A JA8115 are pictured arriving at Heathrow on 8 March 1990.
Jonathan Falconer

Far right:
They say that any landing you can walk away from is a good one, but the arrival on final approach of Boeing 727-2H9 YU-AKJ of Yugoslav operator JAT, trailing a plume of brown smoke and rolling heavily, must have redefined the parameters of passenger comfort for the unfortunates onboard.
Jonathan Falconer

Left:
The new face of Terminal 3 after a four-year modernisation programme costing £110 million. *BAA*

Left:

Concorde G-BOAC undergoes a brief hydraulic systems test before it is towed to Terminal 4 from the airline's maintenance area to operate the 19.00hrs service to New York's John F. Kennedy Airport on 27 April 1990. *Jonathan Falconer*

Below and right:

An atmosphere of tasteful opulence pervades the British Airways Speedwing Lounge at Terminal 4 where passengers for Concorde and First Class intercontinental subsonic flights can relax before boarding. Passengers can watch through the panoramic blind-draped windows as Concorde is readied for departure. *Jonathan Falconer*

Far left:
Nocturne in gold: British Airways' Concorde G-BOAB is pictured at Terminal 4 where she is receiving approximately 86,000kg of JET-A1 to see her safely across the North Atlantic with the 19.00hr departure to New York's John F. Kennedy Airport on 7 December 1989.
Jonathan Falconer

Left:
In this unusual nose-on shot, Concorde G-BOAD is seen undergoing a Major maintenance check during January 1989, which is undertaken every 12,000 flying hours at British Airways' Hatton Cross engineering base. In a complex operation lasting approximately two months, the aircraft is completely stripped of all paint and fittings to enable a thorough inspection of the main structure and components. To give some idea of the amount of work involved, the Major check alone on the pair of intakes for Concorde's Rolls-Royce/ SNECMA Olympus 593-610 turbojets takes the same amount of time as an Intercheck for a complete Boeing 757.
Jonathan Falconer

Right:
The A30 road passes uncomfortably beneath the approach to Runway 27L at Hatton Cross where it often seems possible to reach up and touch inbound aircraft on the last few seconds of their journies to Heathrow . . .

Far right:
. . . a TWA Boeing 747-131 shatters the peace of a Sunday morning in Hounslow . . .

. . . while minutes later El Al's Boeing 747-258B 4X-AXA thunders over the Runway 27R localiser on the last leg of its journey from Tel Aviv.
Jonathan Falconer/Allan Burney

Left:
Attempting to park one's car on a busy high street on a Saturday morning can be a hazardous affair. Pity, then, the pilot of a Boeing 747 who has to manoeuvre an aircraft with a wingspan of 195ft 8in, a length of 231ft 10in, and a height of 63ft 5in to within a few inches of a passsenger loading bridge.

Thanks to a device called the Safegate Docking Guidance System his task is not as impossible as it seems. From an electronic display board mounted on the terminal building the pilot can tell that the gate has been correctly programmed for his type of aircraft, and which aircraft door will be connected to the loading bridge. Inductive sensors buried in the concrete along the parking centreline are activated by pressure from the aircraft's nosewheel gear in the final 12m of its approach to the 'STOP' position. This position is determined by a microcomputer programmed with the correct data for each aircraft type likely to use the gate. As the wheels pass over the sensors the display board indicates the correct stopping position.

British Airways' Boeing 747-236B G-BDXE is pictured on its parking stand at Terminal 4 having successfully completed this crucial manoeuvre.

Jonathan Falconer

Right:

More than 80% of air cargo now travels in passenger aircraft and can be transported from the Central Area passenger terminals to the Cargo Centre on the airport's southside through the cargo road tunnel beneath Runway 27L/09R. The Cargo Centre boasts 94,000sq m of bonded transit shed space built and owned by 16 airlines together with an additional 16,150sq m of bonded transit shed space on the eastern perimeter.

Air Canada's Boeing 747-233B C-GAGB is unloaded at Terminal 3 while ground staff refuel the aircraft with over 150,000 litres of JET-A1 in preparation for the journey home.
BAA/Arthur Kemsley

Far right:

In addition to engineering and maintenance commitments to its own fleet, British Airways also undertakes engineering support and routine maintenance for a number of other airlines, and also for the RAF's TriStar fleet. At the end of the 1980s the total value of engineering work carried out by the airline for outside customers exceeded £70 million per annum.

South African Airways' Boeing 747-344 ZS-SAU, one of two operated by the airline, is pictured at Hatton Cross in January 1989. *Jonathan Falconer*

Right:
Terminal 4's position away from the Central Area is an added headache to the Ground Movement Planner up in the Control Tower. When arriving or departing aircraft use Runways 27R/09L they must cross an active runway — either 27L or 09R.

From the £200 million Terminal 4, British Airways operates its supersonic Concorde services in addition to its long-haul, Paris and Amsterdam services.
BAA/Arthur Kemsley

Below right:
Aeroflot is the world's largest airline and operates the Ilyushin Il-86 — the Soviet Union's first 'airbus' type wide-body — on scheduled services from Moscow to Heathrow, and 14 other overseas destinations.
Peter J. Cooper

Far right:
Little and large: an Iraqi Airways 747-270 and a Lufthansa 727-230 queue for their turn to use the take-off runway. With a high frequency of daily air transport movements, Heathrow's taxiways are somewhat akin to a cab rank with a constant stream of aircraft awaiting their turn to slot into the take-off pattern.
Allan Burney

Far left:

Field Aircraft Services Ltd on the airport's southern perimeter provides hangarage, maintenance and engineering support for a number of private operators, exemplified here by Shell Aircraft Ltd's HS125-700B G-BHSU. *Jonathan Falconer*

Above left:

Early morning getaway: Beecham International Aviation's HS125-600 G-BCXF was used for some years to transport company executives to destinations in Europe, North Africa and the Middle East from Heathrow's executive jet centre. The Aircraft Operator's Certificate held by Beecham enabled the aircraft to be chartered for business trips by other companies without the benefit of owning their own executive aircraft. In its time, 'X-Ray Foxtrot' has carried royalty, rock groups, film stars and politicians, but since the merger of Beecham with the US pharmaceutical giant Smith Kline Beckman in April 1989, the aircraft has been operated on behalf of the new company, Smith Kline Beecham, by Aravco. *Jonathan Falconer*

Below left:

Inside information: Beecham's HS125 has a crew of two pilots and a stewardess, and can carry up to eight passengers. Despite the dated appearance of the aircraft by design standards of the nineties, the HS125 was the first business aircraft to meet jetliner standards of structural safety and operational reliability set by the CAA and FAA. *Jonathan Falconer*

Right:
Visiting aircraft to the General Aviation Centre can often be found parked at British Airways' engineering base nearby. Gulfstream II P2-PNG belongs to the Papua New Guinea government. *Peter J. Cooper*

Below right:
French regional carrier Brit Air frequently operates scheduled passenger services to Heathrow on behalf of Air France and Air Inter from destinations in Normandy and Brittany. Pictured at Heathrow on 14 May 1988, Saab SF340A F-GHDB, operated jointly by Air France and Brit Air, arrives with a mid-morning flight from Nantes. The SF340 carries a flight crew of two and up to 35 passengers seated three abreast with an offset aisle configuration. *Bill Blanchard*

Far right:
Probably one of the quietest aircraft to use Heathrow, British Midland's BAe ATPs are used on short internal feeder flights to Birmingham International and East Midlands Airports. *Allan Burney*

Far right inset:
As well as being the starting point for tens of thousands of flights, a sizeable amount of airliners overfly the London area en route from Europe to the USA and vice versa, without taking off or landing in the UK. The contrails of such overflights are a common sight over the Heathrow area on clear days; these contrails, teased apart by high altitude winds, have been made by aircraft heading north during May 1989.
Jonathan Falconer

Far left and left:
Japan Air Lines is the largest operator of Boeing 747 aircraft in the world, operating an extensive network of scheduled passenger and cargo services to some 34 countries worldwide. JAL is aided in its cargo operation by a fleet of nine Boeing 747-200 freighters.
BAA/Arthur Kemsley

Right:

McDonnell Douglas DC-8 freighters are used by a number of dedicated cargo airlines for medium and long-haul operations. Spanish operator Cargosur is a relative newcomer to the airfreight scene but its DC-8 freighters can occasionally be seen at Heathrow's Cargo Centre, exemplified here in March 1989 by DC-8-62AF EC-230 (later EC-EMX). *Robbie Shaw*

Below right:

The first all-cargo airline in the USA and until recently the World's largest air cargo operator, Flying Tiger Line operated regular scheduled cargo services from New York to Heathrow and Frankfurt using Boeing 747 freighters which were a common sight at the Cargo Centre with their distinctive natural metal finish. In August 1989 FTL was absorbed by Federal Express, its fleet of 747s gradually being repainted into Fed Ex's blue livery and titles. *Robbie Shaw*

Far right:

Federal Express Corporation specialises in door-to-door express delivery of packages and documents. From its operations centre at Memphis International Airport the company operates an extensive network of cargo services to every major market in the USA. Since 1986, Brussels and London have been added to the airline's network of links in 85 countries worldwide. Pictured is DC-10-30AF N315FE, one of a fleet of some 24 DC-10-10 and DC-10-30s operated by the airline. *Allan Burney*

This page:

Named after a character in a fanciful poem by the Russian poet Pushkin, the Antonov An-124 *Ruslan* was, until the appearance of the An-225 *Mriya*, the world's largest and heaviest aircraft. Designed for simultaneous nose and tail loading, the An-124 features a fly-by-wire control system, titanium freight hold floor and a generous use of composite materials in its construction. A rare visitor to Heathrow, Aeroflot's An-124 CCCP-82008 waits at the head of Runway 27R for its take-off clearance on 31 May 1989. *Peter J. Cooper*

Right:

Iraqi Ilyushin Il-76 freighters are frequent visitors to Heathrow. Some 30 of the military M and MD variants are operated by Iraqi Airways, exemplified here by Il-76MD YI-ALU. Both versions feature a rear turret which contains two 23mm cannon, provision for which can be seen in this photograph. In the background can be seen one of Pan Am's Boeing 737-200s which were replaced on the airline's European feeder routes during 1986 by the Boeing 727. *Peter J. Cooper*

Appendix 1

Heathrow's Top 10 Airlines: 1988-89

(ranked by number of passengers carried)

Airline	Passengers carried (× 1,000)	% of total
British Airways	17,114.5	45.0
Pan Am	2,181.7	5.7
British Midland	2,071.2	5.4
Air France	1,614.7	4.2
Aer Lingus	1,418.0	3.7
Lufthansa	1,215.5	3.2
Iberia	1,096.0	2.9
TWA	1,048.7	2.8
Swissair	849.0	2.2
Air Canada	745.4	2.0
Other airlines (total)	8,703.3	22.9
Total	**38,058.0**	**100.0**

Appendix 2

Air Transport Movements by Type at Heathrow: 1988-89

Aircraft type	Movements	% of total
Wide-bodied		
Boeing 747	35,582	11.5
Douglas DC-10	2,189	0.7
Lockheed TriStar	14,428	4.6
Boeing 767	2,058	0.7
Airbus 300	10,493	3.4
Airbus 310	14,549	4.7
Airbus 320	6	*
Long-haul narrow bodied		
Boeing 707/720	2,122	0.7
Douglas DC-8	392	0.1
Short-haul jets		
Boeing 757	44,921	14.5
Boeing 727	18,900	6.1
BAC One-Eleven	18,368	5.9
BAe 146	1,215	0.4
Boeing 737	71,756	23.1
Fokker F-28	6,610	2.1
Douglas DC-9/MD-80	41,145	13.3
Caravelle	25	*
Larger turboprops		
Fokker F-27	4,848	1.6
Vickers Viscount	599	0.2
Handley Page Herald	266	0.1
BAe 748	54	*
DHC Dash-7	2,235	0.7
Smaller turboprops		
Embraer Bandeirante	84	*
Twin Otter	616	0.2
Shorts 330/360	9,070	2.9
BN Islander	43	*
Concorde	2,146	0.7
Other types (Fixed-wing and Helicopters)	5,715	1.8
Grand Total	**310,435**	**100.0**

* Less than 0.1%

Extracted from BAA Airports Traffic Statistics 1988-89 *(Development Planning and Research, British Airport Services Ltd, June 1989)*

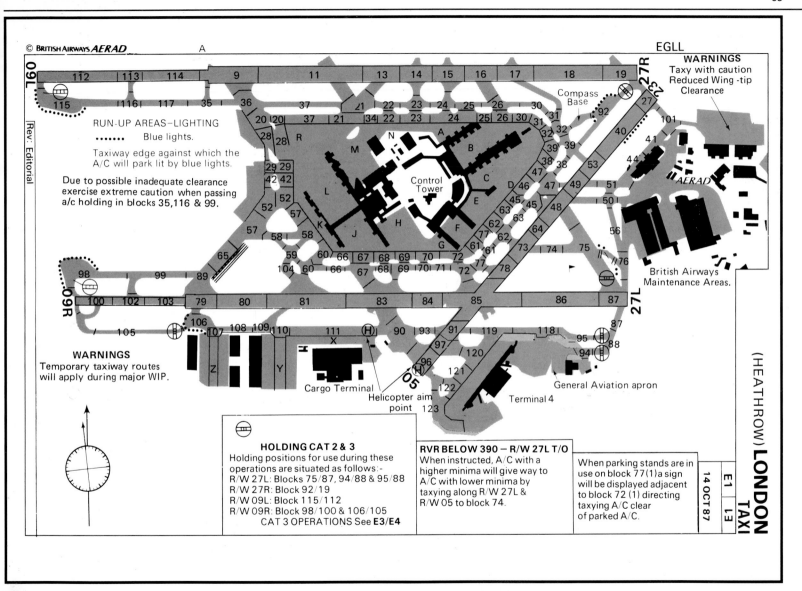

© BRITISH AIRWAYS *AERAD*   A

EGLL

WARNINGS
Taxy with caution
Reduced Wing-tip
Clearance

RUN-UP AREAS–LIGHTING
...... Blue lights.

Taxiway edge against which the
A/C will park lit by blue lights.

Due to possible inadequate clearance
exercise extreme caution when passing
a/c holding in blocks 35,116 & 99.

Compass Base

Control Tower

AERAD

British Airways
Maintenance Areas.

WARNINGS
Temporary taxiway routes
will apply during major WIP.

Cargo Terminal

Helicopter aim
point

General Aviation apron

Terminal 4

Rev. Editorial

HOLDING CAT 2 & 3
Holding positions for use during these
operations are situated as follows:-
R/W 27L: Blocks 75/87, 94/88 & 95/88
R/W 27R: Block 92/19
R/W 09L: Block 115/112
R/W 09R: Block 98/100 & 106/105
CAT 3 OPERATIONS See **E3/E4**

RVR BELOW 390 – R/W 27L T/O
When instructed, A/C with a
higher minima will give way to
A/C with lower minima by
taxying along R/W 27L &
R/W 05 to block 74.

When parking stands are in
use on block 77(1)a sign
will be displayed adjacent
to block 72 (1) directing
taxying A/C clear
of parked A/C.

14 OCT 87   E1   L3

(HEATHROW) **LONDON** TAXI